Christmas Blessings

A COMPILATION OF CHRISTMAS THOUGHTS

© 2023 by Olive Wilson (including all photos unless otherwise stated)

Cover photo: Image by Bruno from Pixabay

Published by Olive Wilson

Edited by Hannah Booth

All rights reserved. No part of this publication may be reproduced, stored in a retrieval system, or transmitted in any form or by any means – for example, electronic, photocopy, recording – without the prior written permission of the publisher. Brief quotations are permitted in printed reviews without the prior permission of the publisher.

Scripture quotations are taken from the New King James Version®. Copyright © 1982 by Thomas Nelson unless otherwise labelled.

ISBN-13: 979-8-8672-6009-5

Dedication

This booklet is dedicated to all who love Christmas!

To
Tony
Merry Christmas
from Wendy
2023

Preface

The musings in this booklet are to help us reflect on the reason for Christmas. While many of us remember Christ's coming into the world in our worship throughout the year, this special time helps us focus on the significance of this miraculous event that took place in the land of Israel two millennia ago.

It is also a compilation of Bible verses, quotes and thoughts from various writers, illustrated with Christmas photographs taken mainly in Cyprus.

Beautiful Christmas lights dotted throughout our cities and streets remind us that Christ, the Light of the World, was born! The words prophesied by Zacharias, father of John the Baptist, have been fulfilled by the *Dayspring from on high*: He has given His light to the thousands of souls who have believed on Him.

And you, child, will be called the prophet of the Highest; for you will go before the face of the Lord to prepare His ways, to give knowledge of salvation to His people by the remission of their sins, through the tender mercy of our God, with which the Dayspring from on high has visited us; to give light to those who sit in darkness and the shadow of death, to guide our feet into the way of peace.

Luke 1:76-79

... the light has come into the world.

John 3:19

And she brought forth her firstborn Son, and wrapped Him in swaddling cloths, and laid Him in a manger, because there was no room for them in the inn.

Luke 2:7

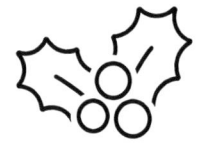

While we enjoy family cheer at Christmas in the comfort of our cosy homes, we remember that the Christ Child was born in the outside place because there was no room for Him in the inn. A cold, uninviting manger/feeding trough was His bed as Mary wrapped Him in swaddling cloths and laid Him there. What a humble start to His days on earth!

Christ's birth impacted the course of history like no other because of who He was and why He came. The Bible records the words proclaimed to Joseph by the Angel of the Lord concerning Mary and the Lord's birth:

She will give birth to a Son, and you shall name Him Jesus (The LORD is salvation), for He will save His people from their sins. Matthew 1:21 (Amplified Bible)

As the angels announced His arrival to the lowly shepherds that holy night in Bethlehem, God's great redeeming plan for reconciliation and peace had commenced on earth. Christ the Lord would bring salvation to all who believe in Him through His sacrificial death on the cross.

Do not be afraid, for behold, I bring you good tidings of great joy which will be to all people. For there is born to you this day in the city of David a Saviour, who is Christ the Lord!

Luke 2:10 -11

After His death, burial and resurrection, Christianity was ignited on the Day of Pentecost when the Holy Spirit came down to earth and into the lives of Christ's followers.

This belief, which has grown exponentially throughout the world, is not a mere 'religion' but a living faith, bringing eternal hope and enlightenment to those in darkness.

Jesus said, *"I am the light of the world. He who follows Me shall not walk in darkness, but have the light of life."*

John 8:12

(image by Kellogem, Pixabay)

A light to bring revelation to the Gentiles, and the glory of Your people Israel.

Luke 2:32

When the Light of the World was born, there was much joy. A vast, heavenly host appeared beside the Angel of the Lord and burst forth in praise, saying:

Glory to God in the highest, and on earth peace, good will toward men! Luke 2:14

This is heaven's wish for mankind, **peace** and **good will**. It starts in hearts who worship the King of Glory and perform God's will on earth until He returns to bring Millennium peace to our broken world.

> *Joy to the world, the Lord is come!*
> *Let earth receive her king;*
> *Let every heart prepare Him room,*
> *And Heaven and nature sing,*
> *And Heaven and nature sing,*
> *And Heaven, and Heaven, and nature sing.*
>
> *Joy to the earth, the Savior reigns!*
> *Let men their songs employ;*
> *While fields and floods, rocks, hills, and plains*
> *Repeat the sounding joy,*
> *Repeat the sounding joy,*
> *Repeat, repeat, the sounding joy.*
>
> *He rules the world with truth and grace*
> *And makes the nations prove*
> *The glories of His righteousness*
> *And wonders of His love*
> *And wonders of His love*
> *And wonders, wonders, of His love.*

Isaac Watts

Joy is the serious business of heaven.

C. S. Lewis

And when they had come into the house, they saw the young Child with Mary His mother, and fell down and worshipped Him. And when they had opened their treasures, they presented gifts to Him: gold, frankincense, and myrrh.

Matthew 2:11

Remember, if Christmas isn't found in your heart, you won't find it under a tree.

Charlotte Carpenter

The vivid red poinsettias, which stand out against the azure skies of Cyprus, not only add colour to the Christmas decorations but also have a poignant symbolic meaning.

The star shape in the centre resembles the star of Bethlehem and the leafy red bracts represent the blood of Christ, a visible reminder of the reason for His coming.

In Him we have redemption through His blood, the forgiveness of sins, according to the riches of His grace.

Ephesians 1:7

I live by faith in the Son of God, who loved me and gave Himself for me.

Galatians 2:20

You can never truly enjoy Christmas until you can look up into the Father's face and tell Him you have received His Christmas gift.

John R. Rice

🙶

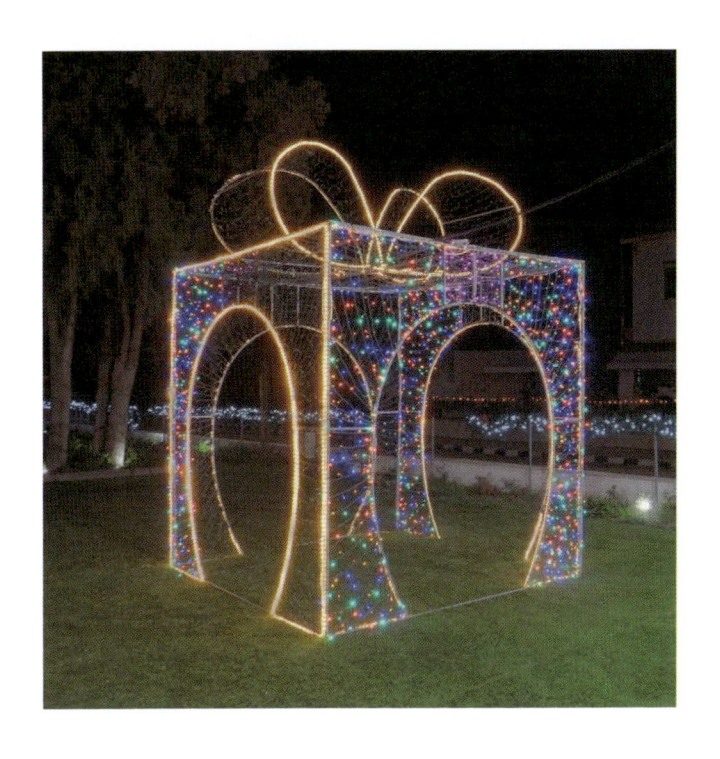

Thanks be to God for his indescribable gift!

2 Corinthians 9:15

What can I give Him, poor as I am?
If I were a shepherd, I would bring a lamb;
If I were a Wise Man, I would do my part;
Yet what I can I give Him: give my heart.

(From 'In the Bleak Midwinter')

Every good gift and every perfect gift is from above, and comes down from the Father of lights ...
> James 1:17

The significance of the Christian faith, which commenced with Christ's birth, cannot be overstated. Renowned author and apologist, C. S. Lewis, wrote:

Christianity, if false, is of no importance, and if true, of infinite importance. The only thing it cannot be is moderately important.

The Christmas story may read like a fable, but it has often been said that truth is stranger than fiction. The story's Author, Omnipotent God, created and upholds the billions of galaxies in our universe. God came to us in the form of a human being at Christmas to do His Father's will on earth and bring life to all mankind.

The words of C. S. Lewis provoke the reader to assess the validity of the Christian faith and its crucial message, which first echoed in the Judean hills. We are challenged to apply the message personally to our lives by seeking salvation from the living Christ. May we discover that Christianity is true and therefore of *infinite importance*!

Our outlook can be altered by viewing the facts from a new perspective. God wants to bless us with the gift of His great love and to guide us in His peace.

For I know the thoughts that I think toward you, says the Lord, thoughts of peace and not of evil, to give you a future and a hope. Jeremiah 29:11

The truth of Christmas will change our hearts and eternal destination when we accept it. As we reflect with perhaps a renewed understanding of why the Son of Man came to earth, may we make Him Lord of our lives. He offers us forgiveness of sins through repentance and faith.

"I will honour Christmas in my heart, and try to keep it all the year."

A Christmas Carol

🙶

I heard the bells on Christmas Day
Their old familiar carols play,
And wild and sweet,
the words repeat
Of peace on earth, good-will to men!

H. W. Longfellow

The aromas and memories of Christmas are sweet to us if we have lived in freedom and peace. However, we take a moment to remember war-torn countries and families who have lost members through the brutality of war.

There will be many empty places at tables this year, and in many instances, families have been displaced and cannot celebrate in their usual way. We can pray for the Lord's comfort amidst the hurt and tragedy of war.

The Christmas truce of 1914 during World War 1 was made famous 100 years later by Sainsbury's Christmas advertisement: when a British soldier hears the carol 'Silent Night' being sung in the German trenches, he tentatively approaches enemy lines, and a truce is made. After an exchange of gifts and a game of football, the soldiers return to their respective sides, having experienced the power of the true Christmas spirit.

May you have a peaceful Christmas celebration with family and friends and know the presence of Christ's Spirit in the coming year!

Merry Christmas and a Happy New Year!

Who can add to Christmas? The perfect motive is that God so loved the world. The perfect gift is that He gave His only Son. The only requirement is to believe in Him. The reward of faith is that you shall have everlasting life.

Corrie ten Boom

For unto us a Child is born, unto us a Son is given; and the government will be upon His shoulder. And His name will be called Wonderful, Counsellor, Mighty God, Everlasting Father, Prince of Peace.

Isaiah 9:6

Printed in Great Britain
by Amazon